CONTENTS

Granny Square Techniques

GETTING STARTED

Most granny squares are worked in rounds, beginning with a center ring. There are different ways to begin the ring. The method you choose may depend on whether you want the center to be open or tightly closed.

CHAIN RING

In this method the size of the ring is fixed and cannot be tightened.

1. Make a foundation chain, joining with a slip stitch to form a ring.

2. Work the next round inserting the hook into the center of the ring rather than in the chain stitches.

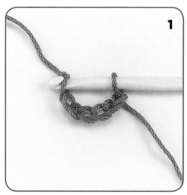 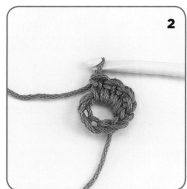

SLIP KNOT

1. Form a loose slip knot. Holding the tail between your thumb and middle finger, work the first round of stitches into the slip knot.

2. Before joining the round, gently pull the tail of the knot to tighten the center.

ADJUSTABLE RING

A third method, sometimes referred to as magic ring or sliding loop, also allows you to pull the ring tightly closed.

1. Wrap the yarn clockwise around your index finger twice, leaving a 6" (15.2 cm) tail. Holding the tail between your thumb and middle finger, slide the hook under the wraps and catch the working yarn.

2. Pull the working yarn through the ring, and chain the designated number of stitches.

3. Work additional stitches into the two loops of the ring, keeping the tail free. Before joining the round, pull on the tail a little; one loop will tighten slightly. Pull on that loop, which will tighten the other loop.

4. Then pull the tail to tighten the remaining loop.

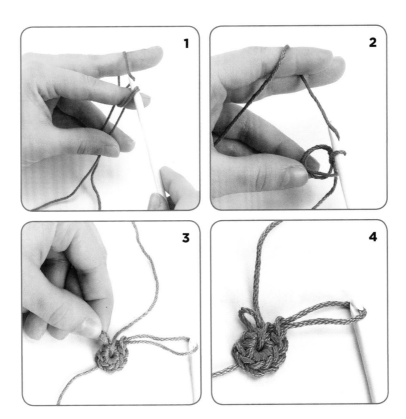

CLASSIC GRANNY SQUARE

Most granny squares are worked in rounds instead of rows. A classic granny begins with a foundation chain formed in a circle. Because many of the floral granny squares in this book are very textural, you may find it appealing to separate them with the plainer classic granny squares for projects like blankets. If you have never crocheted a granny square before, this is the best place to start!

HOW TO CROCHET A CLASSIC GRANNY SQUARE

1. Foundation rnd: With A, ch 4, join with a Sl st to form a ring.

2. **RND 1:** With A, ch 3 (counts as a dc), work 2 more dc in ring, *ch 3, work 3 more dc in ring, rep from * twice more, join with a Sl st to 3rd ch of beg ch 3.

3. **RND 2:** Join B by making a slip knot on hook, place hook in any corner ch-3 sp, pick up a loop, yo through 2 (1 ch made), ch 2 more for beg chain (A). 2 dc in same ch-3 sp (half corner made), *ch 2 [3 dc, ch 3, 3 dc] in next ch-3 sp (corner made) (B), rep from * twice, ch 2, 3 dc in same sp as beg ch-3, ch 3, join with a Sl st to 3rd ch of beg ch-3 (C).

4. **RND 3:** Join A with a slip knot (same as rnd 2), make 2 more dc in same ch 3 sp (half corner made), *ch 2, 3 dc in next ch-2 sp, ch 2, [3 dc, ch 3, 3 dc] in next ch-3 sp (corner made), rep from * twice, ch 2, 3 dc in next ch-2 sp, ch 2, 3 dc in same sp as beg half corner, ch 3, join with a Sl st to 3rd ch of beg ch-3, fasten off.

Continue to add rounds until your classic granny square is the size you desire. Here is a Classic Granny with four rounds. Refer to the symbol chart on page 32 if you are unfamiliar with reading crochet stitch diagrams.

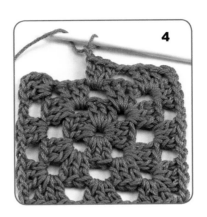

BEGINNING CHAINS

When you crochet in rows, you alternate from right side to wrong side with each row. At the end of each row, you crochet a turning chain of one to four chains, depending on the height of the next row of stitches. When crocheting granny squares, you are working in rounds always from the right side and continuing in the same direction, but you still crochet a chain to begin the round. If the next round will be single crochet, you chain 1 to begin; half-double crochet: chain 2; double crochet: chain 3; triple crochet: chain 4, etc. The directions will tell you how many chains to make. The beginning chain counts as a stitch. For instance, the directions may say, "ch 3 (counts as dc)." At the end of each round, the last stitch is worked into the beginning chain from the previous round.

INVISIBLE JOIN

When working in the round, connecting the end of the round to the beginning can sometimes seem awkward. Here is a way to connect the last stitch in a way that will leave the connection nearly invisible.

1. End the last stitch but do not join to the beginning with a slip stitch.

2. Cut the yarn, leaving a tail several inches long. Pull the yarn through the last stitch and set the hook aside. Thread the tail on a tapestry needle, and run the needle under the beginning stitch, pulling the tail through.

3. Insert the needle back through the center of the last stitch of the round and pull the tail to the back of the work (not too tightly).

4. This will join the beginning to the end invisibly. Weave the tail into the back of the work.

GAUGE AND ADJUSTING SIZES

Every pattern will tell you the exact yarn (or weight of yarn) to use, and suggest what size hook to use to crochet an item with the same finished measurements as the project shown. It is important to choose yarn in the weight specified in order to successfully complete the project. The hook size recommended is the size an average crocheter would use to get the correct gauge. Gauge refers to the number of stitches and the number of rows in a given width and length, usually in 4" (10 cm), of crocheted fabric. For this book, gauge also refers to the finished size of a granny square.

Before beginning to crochet a project, it is very important to take the time to check your gauge, whether you use the yarn specified or substitute another yarn of the same weight. This is especially important for garments or projects that must be specific dimensions. Crochet a sample swatch of the stitch pattern or crochet one of the granny squares used in the project. If you have more stitches to the inch or if your square is smaller than the instructions call for, you are working tighter than average; try a new swatch or square with a larger hook. If you have fewer stitches to the inch or if your square is larger than the instructions call for, you are working looser than average; try a smaller hook. Always change hook size to get proper gauge, rather than trying to work tighter or looser.

These three samples of the same granny square were worked on different yarns with different size hooks. You can see why working to the correct gauge makes a huge difference in the finished size of your project.

SEAMS

Once you have crocheted all the granny squares for a project, you join them into one large piece using one of several methods. For some methods you sew seams with yarn and a tapestry needle. For other methods, you use a crochet hook. Some might consider this final step of a project to be a chore, but to me, the rhythm of hand sewing is soothing and relaxing.

WHIPSTITCH SEAM

The whipstitch seam works best for sewing straight-edged seams. This method creates a little decorative ridge on the right side of work. Place two squares side-by-side, wrong-side up, aligning the stitches of the outer round. Insert the needle through the top loops of corresponding stitches, bring through and around, and repeat.

WRONG SIDE

RIGHT SIDE

WEAVE SEAM

Use this join when you want a really flat seam. Hold pieces to be seamed side-by-side and, working from the wrong side, insert needle from front to back, through 1 loop only, draw through, progress to next stitch, bring needle from back to front (not over), and proceed in this manner until seam is completed. If you draw through top loop only, a decorative ridge will be left on the right side of work. If you draw through bottom loops, the ridge will be on the back of the work.

WRONG SIDE

RIGHT SIDE

SINGLE CROCHET SEAM

The single crochet seam creates a decorative ridge. Holding the pieces wrong sides together, work single crochet through the whole stitch on both motifs.

WRONG SIDE

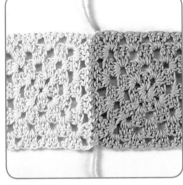

RIGHT SIDE

CHAIN JOIN

When the outer rounds of your squares have open spaces, you can join pieces with a stitch pattern that suits the spacing. This decorative join can be worked from either side. Place the pieces right sides together (or wrong sides together), aligning the stitches. Join yarn in one corner through both layers. *Chain 3, skip 3, single crochet through spaces of both layers, repeat from *.

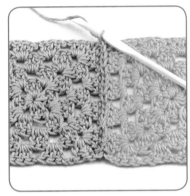

WRONG SIDE

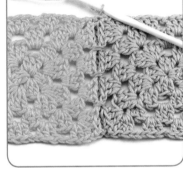

RIGHT SIDE

LACY CHAIN SEAM

This method of joining granny squares creates a more open seam, resulting in a lighter weight, lacy look.

Hold two squares together, one above the other, join yarn in corner space on bottom square, ch 3 remove hook from loop, place hook in corner of top granny square, pick up dropped loop and pull through, *ch 3, skip 2 sts on bottom square, 1 sc in next st, ch 3, skip 2 sts on top square, remove hook from ch, put hook through the next st, pick up dropped loop and pull through st, repeat from * end last sc in bottom corner, ch 3, remove hook, place hook in top corner, pick up dropped loop and pull through, fasten off.

BORDERS

You often need to pick up stitches from the edges of a crocheted piece to add a border. When picking up stitches along the sides of granny squares, simply pick up one stitch for every stitch along the edge.

Picking up stitches along row ends of a crocheted piece is a little more complex. The general rule of thumb is to pick up one stitch in every other row for single crochet (1). For instance, if you have worked twenty rows of single crochet, you will pick up ten stitches along the row ends. Pick up one stitch for every row for double crochet (2). For instance, if you have worked twenty rows of double crochet, you will pick up twenty stitches. These guidelines work most of the time, but not always. Your work must lie flat, and sometimes you will have to experiment to judge how to proceed. If your edges are rippling, like a ruffle, you are picking up too many stitches; if they are pulling in, you are picking up too few stitches.

The best way to get an even edge is to divide the length to be worked into four parts. When the first section is done and lies flat, repeat that number of stitches for each of the following three sections. Work in every stitch of the top and bottom edges. Always work three stitches in each corner to make the project lie flat.

Granny Square Patterns

The twelve granny square patterns included in this book represent the traditional flowers of each month. Instructions are provided in written rounds and in stitch symbol diagrams. All of the samples have been crocheted in the same lightweight cotton yarn with the same size hook to make the variations in the stitch patterns most apparent. Vary the colors, fibers, and weights of yarn to make squares with different characteristics.

FLOWERS OF THE MONTH

JANUARY CARNATION

A carnation expresses love; also a friend in adversity.

SKILL LEVEL: Intermediate

Made with 3 colors: A, B, and C.

With A, ch 5, join with a sl st to form a ring.

RND 1: Ch 1, 10 sc in ring, join with a sl st in first sc. (10 sc)

RND 2: Working in front loop only, ch 2 (counts as hdc), 2 hdc in same st, 3 hdc in each of st around, join with a sl st in top of beg ch-2. (30 hdc)

RND 3: Ch 1, sc in first st, ch 3, (sc, ch 3) in each hdc around, join with a sl st in first sc. Fasten off A.

RND 4: With right side facing, working behind sts in Rnd 2, rejoin A in remaining back loop of any sc in Rnd 1, ch 3 (counts as dc), *3 dc in next st** dc in next st; rep from * around, ending last rep at **, join with a sl st in top of beg ch-3. (20 dc)

RND 5: Ch 1, sc in first st, ch 3, (sc, ch 3) in each hdc around, join with a sl st in first sc. Fasten off A.

RND 6: With right side facing, working behind sts in Rnd 5, rejoin A with a sl st in top of ch-3 at beg of Rnd 4, ch 1, sc in first st, ch 3, skip next 3 dc, *sc in next dc, ch 3, skip next 3 dc; rep from * around, join with a sl st in first sc. Fasten off A. (5 ch-3 sps)

RND 7: With right side facing, join B with a sl st in any ch-3 sp, ch 1, sc in ch-3 sp, *ch 10, sl st in first ch from hook, sc next ch, hdc in each of next 8 ch, sc in same ch-3 sp, ch 3**, 1 sc in next ch-3 sp; rep from * around, ending last rep at **, join with a sl st in first sc. Fasten off B. (5 leaves, 5 ch-3 sps)

RND 8: With right side facing, join C with a sl st in any ch-3 sp, ch 3 (counts as dc), 2 dc in same sp, dc in next sc, *ch 4, working behind next leaf, 3 dc in next ch-3 sp, dc in next sc; rep from * around, ch 4, join with a sl st in top of beg ch-3. (20 dc; 5 ch-5 sps)

RND 9: Ch 3 (counts as dc), dc in each next 3 dc, 4 dc in next ch-4 sp, dc in each of the next 2 dc, ch 3 (corner), dc in each of next 2 dc, 4 dc in next ch-4 sp, dc in each of next 4 dc, ch 3 (corner), 4 dc in next ch-4 sp, dc in each of next 4 dc, (2 dc, ch 3 [corner], 2 dc) in next ch-4 sp, dc in each of next 4 dc, 4 dc in last ch-4 sp, ch 3 (corner), join with a sl st in top of beg ch-3. Fasten off C. (10 dc on each side; 4 corner ch-3 sps)

RND 10: With right side facing, join A with a sl st in any corner ch-3 sp, *(3 sc, ch-2, 3 sc) in corner sp, *sc in each of next 10 sc; rep from * around, join with a sl st in first sc. Fasten off A. (16 sc on each side)

RND 11: With right side facing, join B in any corner ch-2 sp, ch 3 (counts as dc) (dc, ch 2, 2 dc) in same sp, *ch 1, sk next sc, dc in each of next 2 sc, [ch-2, sk 2 sc, dc in each of next 2] 3 times, ch 1, sk next sc** (2 dc, ch 2, 2 dc) in next ch-2 sp (corner); rep from * around, ending last rep at **, join with a sl st in top of beg ch-3. Fasten off.

FEBRUARY VIOLET

Violets express modesty, faithfulness, virtue, and young love.

SKILL LEVEL: Intermediate

Made with 4 colors: A, B, C, and D.

Picot: Ch 3, sl st in 3rd ch from hook.

With A, ch 4, join with a sl st to form a ring.

RND 1: Ch 1, 10 sc in ring. (10 sc)

RND 2: Ch 1, sc in first st, *(sl st, ch 3, tr, picot, tr, ch 3, sl st) in next sc, sc in next sc; rep from * twice, ch 2, (2 dc, ch 2, sl st) in next sc, sl st in next sc, ch 2, (2 dc, ch 2, sl st) in next sc, join with a sl st in first sc. (3 large petals, 2 small petals)

RND 3: Working behind petals, ch 1, sc in first sc, *ch 5, sk next petal**, sc in next st between petals; rep from * around, ending last rep at **, ch 5, join with a sl st in first sc. Fasten off A. (5 ch-5 loops)

RND 4: With right side facing, join B with a sl st in any sc between petals, ch 1, sc in first sc, *ch 2, (2 dc, tr, picot, tr, 2 dc) in next ch-5 sp, ch 2**, sc in next sc; rep from * around, ending last rep at **, join with a sl st in first sc. (5 leaves)

RND 5: Ch 1, sc in first sc, working behind leaves, *ch 7, skip next leaf**, sc in next sc between leaves; rep from *, ending last rep at **, join with a sl st in first sc. Fasten off B. (5 ch-7 loops)

RND 6: With right side facing, join C in any ch-7 loop, ch 3 (cts as a dc) 9 more dc in same loop [10 dc in next ch-7 loop] 4 times, join with a sl st to 3rd ch of beg ch-3. (50 dc)

RND 7: Ch 1, 1 sc in each dc around. (50 sc)

RND 8: Ch 3, 2 dc in same st, ch 3, 3 dc in next st (corner), *sk next sc, [sc next sc, ch 1, sk next sc] 5 times, 3 dc in next st, ch 3, 3 dc in next st (corner made), sk next sc [sc in next sc, ch 1, sk next sc] 4 times, sc in next sc*, 3 dc in next sc, ch 3, 3 dc in next st (corner made); rep from * to * once, join with a sl st in top of beg ch-3. Fasten off C. (4 ch-1 sps on each side; 4 corner ch-3 sps)

RND 9: With right side facing, join C with a sl st in any ch-3 corner space, ch 3 (counts as dc) (2 dc, ch 3, 3 dc) in same space, *(ch 1, 2 dc) in each of next 4 ch-1 sps, ch 1**, (3 dc, ch 3, 3 dc) in next ch-3 corner sp; rep from * around, ending last rep at **, join with sl st in top of beg ch-3. Fasten off.

MARCH DAFFODIL

Daffodils express regard, devotion, and affection.

SKILL LEVEL: Intermediate

Made with 4 colors: A, B, C, and D.

BELL

Foundation: With A, ch 12, join with a sl st to form a ring.

RND 1: Ch 1, sc in back loop of each ch around, join with a sl st in first sc. (12 sc)

RND 2: Ch 1, 1 sc in each sc, join with a sl st to beg ch 1.

RND 3: Ch 3 (counts as dc), dc in each sc around, join with a sl st in top of beg ch-3. (12 dc)

RND 4: *Ch 3, sc in 3rd ch from hook for picot, sl st in next dc; rep from * around, join with a sl st in sl st at beg of rnd. Fasten off A. (6 picots)

BACKGROUND

RND 5: Working on opposite side of foundation ch, rejoin A with a sl st in any ch, ch 1, sc in same ch, *ch 3 (tr, ch 3, sl st in 3rd ch from hook for picot, tr) in next ch, ch 3**, sc in next ch; rep from * around, ending last rep at **, join with a sl st in first sc. (6 petals)

RND 6: Ch 1, sc in first sc, *ch 5, sk next petal**, sc in next sc between petals; rep from * around, ending last rep at **, join with a sl st in first sc. Fasten off A. (6 ch-5 loops)

RND 7: With right side facing, join B in any sc between petals, ch 1, sc in first sc, *ch 2, (2 dc, tr, ch 3, sl st in 3rd ch from hook for picot, tr, 2 dc) in next ch-5 loop, ch 2**, sc in next sc; rep from * around, ending last rep at **. (6 leaves)

RND 8: Ch 1, sc in first sc, working behind leaves, *ch 4, sc in next ch-5 loop in Rnd 6, between center 2 tr of Rnd 7, ch 4**, sc in next sc; rep from * around, ending last rep at **, join with a sl st in first sc. Fasten off B. (12 ch-4 loops)

RND 9: With right side facing, join C with a sl st in any ch-4 loop, ch 3 (counts as dc), (2 dc, ch 3, 3 dc) in same loop (corner), *[ch 1, 3 dc in next ch-4 loop] twice, ch 1**, (3 dc, ch 3, 3 dc) in next ch-4 loop (corner); rep from * around, ending last rep at **, join with a sl st in top of beg ch-3. Fasten off C. (4 ch-3 corner sps; 2 groups of 3-dc between corners)

RND 10: With right side facing, join D with a sl st in any ch-3 corner sp, ch 3 (counts as dc), (2 dc, ch 3, 3 dc) in same loop (corner), *[ch 1, 3 dc in next ch-4 loop] 3 times, ch 1**, (3 dc, ch 2, 3 dc) in next ch-4 loop (corner); rep from * around, ending last rep at **, join with a sl st in top of beg ch-3. Fasten off. (4 ch-3 corner sps; 3 groups of 3-dc between corners)

BELL

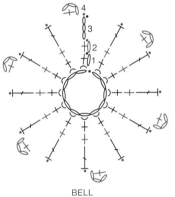

BACKGROUND

APRIL DAISY

The daisy celebrates the arrival of spring, Easter, and Passover.

SKILL LEVEL: Intermediate

Made with 4 colors: A, B, C, and D.

With A, ch 4, join with a sl st to form a ring.

RND 1: Ch 1, 12 sc in ring, join with a sl st in first sc. Fasten off A. (12 sc)

RND 2: With right side facing, join B with a sl st in any sc, ch 1, sc in first sc, *ch 2, (dc, tr, ch 3, tr, dc) in next sc, ch 2**, sc in next sc; rep from * around, join with a sl st in first sc. Fasten off B. (6 petals)

RND 3: With right side facing, join C with a sl st in any sc between petals, ch 6 (counts as tr, ch 3), *sc in the center ch of next ch-3 sp, ch 3**, tr in next sc between 2 petals, ch 3; rep from * around, ending last rep at **, join with a sl st in top of beg ch-3. (12 ch-3 spaces)

RND 4: Ch 1, 2 sc in first st (corner), *[3 sc in next ch-3 sp, sc in next st] twice, 3 sc in next ch-3 sp**, 2 sc in next sc (corner); rep from * around, ending last repeat at **, join with a sl st in first sc. (52 sc)

RND 5: Ch 3, 2 dc in same st, ch 3 (corner), 3 dc in next st, *sk next sc, [sc in next sc, ch 1, sk next sc] 4 times, sc next sc, sk next sc**, 3 dc in next st, ch 3, 3 dc in next st; rep from * around, ending last rep at **, join with a sl st in top of beg ch-3. Fasten off C. (4 ch-1 sps on each side)

RND 6: With right side facing, join C with a sl st in any ch-3 corner sp, ch 3 (counts as dc), (2 dc, ch 3, 3 dc] in same sp, *[ch 1, 2 dc in next ch-1 space] 4 times, ch 1**, (3 dc, ch 3, 3 dc) in next ch-3 corner sp; rep from * around, ending last rep at **, join with a sl st in top of beg ch-3. Fasten off.

MAY LILY OF THE VALLEY

The Lily of the Valley expresses sweetness, humility, and hope.

SKILL LEVEL: Intermediate

Made with 4 colors: A, B, C, and D

Puff st: [Yo, insert hook an next st, yo, draw up a loop] 3 times in same st, yo, draw yarn through all 7 loops on hook.

Joining leaf: To join leaf, place hook through point of leaf and through designated st or sp, pick up a loop, and complete a sc.

With A, ch 5, join with a sl st to form a ring.

RND 1: Ch 1, 12 sc in ring, join with a sl st in first sc.

RND 2: Ch 3 (counts as dc here and throughout), dc in same st, 2 dc in each sc around. (24 dc)

RND 3: Ch 1, sc in first st, *ch 11, sc in 3rd ch from hook, hdc in each of the next 7 ch, sl st in next ch, ch 1, sk next sc**, sc in next st, rep from *around, ending last rep at **, join with a sl st in first sc. Fasten off A. (8 leaves, 8 ch-1 sps)

RND 4: With right side facing, join B in any ch-1 sp between leaves, working behind leaves, [ch 3, sc in next ch-1 sp] 8 times, join with a sl st in first ch. (8 ch-3 sps)

RND 5: Ch 3, 5 dc in first ch-3 sp, 6 dc in each sp around, join with a sl st in top of beg ch-3. (48 dc)

RND 6: Ch 3, dc in each of the next 11 dc, ch 3 (corner), *dc in each of the next 12 dc, ch 3, rep from * twice, join with a sl st in top of beg ch-3. (12 dc on each side; 4 ch-3 corner sps)

(continued)

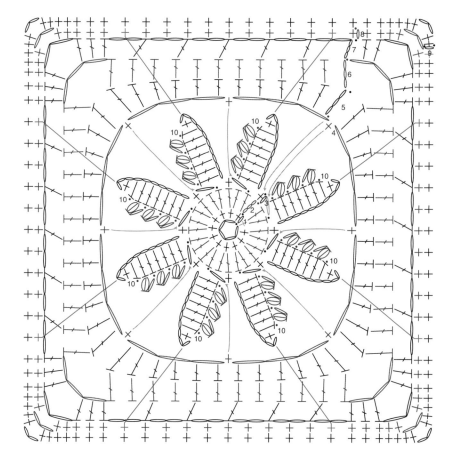

RND 7: Ch 5 (counts as dc, ch 2), sk first 2 dc, [dc next dc, ch 2, sk next st] 5 times, *(3 dc, ch 2, 3 dc) in next ch-3 corner sp, ch 2, sk next 2 sts, [dc in next dc, ch 2, sk next st] 5 times, rep from * twice, (3 dc, ch 3, 2 dc) in next ch-3 corner sp, join with a sl st to 3rd ch of beg ch-3 to complete last corner.

RND 8: Ch 1, sc in first st, *sc in next ch-2 sp, joining leaf, [sc in next dc, 1 sc in ch-2 sp] 4 times, sc in next dc, sc in ch-2 sp, joining leaf, sc in each of next 3 dc, (2 sc, ch 2, 2 sc) in next corner ch-2 sp, sc in each of next 3 dc, rep from * 3 times, join with a sl st in first sc. Fasten off B. (21 sc on each side)

RND 9: With right side facing, join C with a sl st in any ch-2 corner sp, ch 1, (2 sc, ch 2, 2 sc) in ch-2 corner sp, *sc in each of next 21 sc, (2 sc, ch 2, 2 sc) in corner ch-2 sp, repeat from * around, join with a sl st in first sc. Fasten off C.

LILY BLOSSOMS

ROW 10: With right side facing, join D in the first hdc at top of any leaf, *Puff st in next st, yo, draw through all 7 loops on hook, ch-1, sl st in next hdc, rep from * twice. Fasten off D. Rep Row 10 in each leaf around. Fasten off D.

CENTER BLOSSOM

With D, ch 5, join with a sl st to form a ring.

RND 1: Ch 2, 9 hdc in ring, join with an invisible join. Fasten off D, leaving a sewing length. Sew blossom to center of square.

JUNE ROSE

The rose expresses love, devotion, and affection.

SKILL LEVEL: Intermediate

Made with 3 colors: A, B, and C.

With A, ch 4, join with sl st to form a ring.

RND 1: Ch 1, 10 sc in ring, join with a sl st in first sc.

RND 2: Working in front loops only, *ch 2, 3 dc in next st, ch 2, slip st in next st, rep from * 4 times, join with a sl st in first sc of Rnd 1. (5 petals)

RND 3: Working in remaining back loops of Rnd 1, ch 1, sc in first sc, *ch 3, sk 1 st, sc in next st, rep from * 3 times, ch 3, join with a sl st in first sc. (5 ch-3 sps)

RND 4: (Sl st, ch 2, 3 tr, ch 2, sl st) in each ch-3 sp around, sl st in first sc of Rnd 3. (5 petals)

RND 5: Working behind petals, ch 1, sc in first sc of Rnd 3, ch 3, sc in base of third tr of next petal, ch 3**, sc in sc between petals, rep from * around, ending last rep at **, join with a sl st in first sc. Fasten off A. (10 ch-3 sps)

RND 6: With right side facing, join B with a sl st in any ch-3 sp, *(ch 2, hdc, dc, 2 tr, ch 3, 2 tr, dc, hdc, ch 2, sl st) in same ch-3 sp, sc in next ch-3 sp**, sl st in next ch-3 sp, rep from * around, ending last rep at ** once, join with a sl st in first sl st. (5 leaves)

RND 7: Working behind leaves, [ch 7, sc in next sc between leaves] 5 times, ch 7, join with a sl st in first ch. Fasten off B. (5 ch-7 sps)

RND 8: With right side facing, join C with a sl st in any ch-7 sp, ch 3 (does not count as a st), 8 dc in same ch-7 sp, 9 dc in each ch-7 sp around, join with a sl st in top of beg ch-3. (44 dc)

RND 9: Ch 3 (does not count as a st), *(3 dc, ch 3, 3 dc) in next dc (corner), dc in each of the next 10 dc, rep from * around, join with a sl st in first dc. Fasten off C. (16 dc on each side)

RND 10: With right side facing, join A with a sl st in any corner ch-3 sp, ch 3 (counts as dc) (dc, ch 2, 2 dc) in same sp (corner), ch 1, sk next dc, [dc in next 2 sts, ch 2, sk 2 sts] 3 times, dc in next 2 sts, ch 1, sk next dc**, (2 dc, ch 2, 2 dc) in next ch-3 sp (corner), rep from * around, ending last rep at ** , join with a sl st in top of beg ch-3. Fasten off.

JULY WATER LILY

Water lily expresses laughter and purity of heart.

SKILL LEVEL: Intermediate

Made with 3 colors: A, B, and C.

Picot: Ch 4, sc in 4th ch from hook.

Double Treble Crochet (dtr) Yo (3 times), insert hook in designated st or sp, yo, draw up a loop, [yo, through 2 loops on hook] 3 times.

With A, ch 6, join with a sl st to form a ring.

RND 1: Ch 5 (counts as dc, ch 2), [dc, ch 2] 7 times in ring, join with a sl st in 3rd ch of beg ch-5. (8 dc, 8 ch-2 sps)

RND 2: Ch 1, [sc, dc, tr, picot, tr, dc, sc] in ea ch-2 sp around, join with a sl st to first sc, turn. (8 petals)

RND 3: With wrong side facing, ch 1, sc in next dc in Rnd 1, [ch 3, sc in next dc between petals from Rnd 1] 7 times, ch 3, join with a sl st to first sc, turn. Fasten off A. (8 ch-3 sps)

RND 4: With right side facing, join B with a sl st in any ch-3 sp, (sc, 2 dc, tr, picot, tr, 2 dc, sc) in each ch-3 sp around, join with a sl st to first sc, turn. (8 petals)

RND 5: With wrong side facing, ch 1, sc between 2 sc, *ch 4, sk next petal, sc between 2 sc of next 2 petals, rep from * 5 times, ch 4, join with a sl st in first sc, turn. Fasten off B. (8 ch-4 sps)

RND 6: With right side facing, join C with a sl st in any ch-4 sp, (sc, dc, tr, dtr, picot, dtr, tr, dc, sc, ch 1) in each ch-3 sp around, join with a sl st to first sc, turn. (8 leaves)

RND 7: With wrong side facing, working behind leaves, ch 1, sc in next ch-1 sp, *ch 5, sc in next ch-1 sp between petals, rep from * around, join with a sl st in first sc, turn. Fasten off C. (8 ch-5 sps)

RND 8: With right side facing, join D with a sl st in any ch-5 sp, ch 3 (counts as dc here and throughout), 4 dc in same sp, 5 dc in each ch-5 sp round, join with a sl st in top of beg ch-3. (40 dc)

RND 9: Ch 1, sc in first st, sc in each of the next 9 dc, ch 3 (corner), *sc in each of next 10 dc, ch 3 (corner); rep from * around, join with a sl st in first sc. Fasten off D. (10 sc on each side; 4 ch-3 sps)

RND 10: With right side facing, join B with a sl st in any corner ch-3 sp, ch 3, (dc, ch 3, 2 dc) in same corner sp, *[ch 2, sk next sc, dc in each of the next 2 sc] 3 times, ch 2, sk next sc**, (2 dc, ch 3, 2 dc) in next corner ch-3 sp, rep from * around, ending last rep at **, join with a sl st in top of beg ch-3. Fasten off B.

RND 11: With right side facing, join D with a sl st in any ch-3 corner sp, ch 1, *(2 sc, ch 2, 2 sc) in ch-3 corner sp, [sc in each of next 2 dc, 2 sc in next ch-2 sp] 4 times, sc in each of the next 2 dc, rep from * around, join with a sl st in first sc. Fasten off.

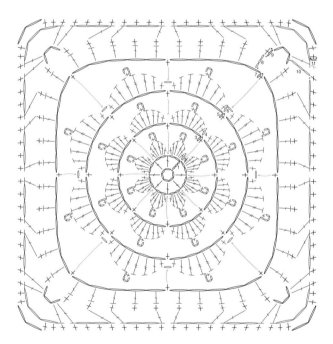

AUGUST POPPY

The poppy expresses strength of character, sincerity, and generosity.

SKILL LEVEL: Intermediate

Made with 5 colors: A, B, C, D, and E.

Picot: Ch 4, sc in 4th ch from hook.

Joining leaf: To join leaf, place hook through point of leaf and through designated st or sp, pick up a loop, and complete a sc.

With A, ch 5, join with a sl st to form a ring.

RND 1: Ch 1, 8 sc in ring, join with a sl st in first sc. Fasten off A.

RND 2: With right side facing, join B with a sl st in any sc, ch 3 (counts as dc here and throughout), dc in first st, *dc in next sc**, 2 dc in next sc, rep from * around, ending last rep at **, join with a sl st top of beg ch-3. Fasten off B. (12 dc)

RND 3: Working in front loops of sts, with right side facing, join C in first st, ch 3, dc in first dc, 2 dc in each dc around, join with a sl st top of beg ch-3. (24 dc)

RND 4: Ch 3, *2 dc next st**, dc next st, rep from * around, ending last rep at **, join with a sl st in top of beg ch-3. (36 dc)

RND 5: Ch 1, sc in first st, ch 3, (sc, ch 3) in each sc around, join with a sl st in first sc. Fasten off C. (36 ch-3 sps)

RND 6: Working in remaining back loops of sts of Rnd 3, with right side facing, join D with a sl st in any dc in Rnd 3, ch 1, sc in first st, *ch 3, sk next 2 sc**, sc in next sc, rep from * around, ending last rep at **, join with a sl st in first sc. (8 ch-3 sps)

RND 7: (Sl st, ch 3, 3 tr, ch 4, picot, 3 tr, ch 3, sl st) in each ch-3 sp around, join with a sl st in first sc of Rnd 6. (8 leaves)

RND 8: Working behind leaves, ch 1, sc in first sc, *ch 6, skip next petal**, sc in next sc in Rnd 6, between leaves, rep from * around, ending last rep at **, join with a sl st to first sc. Fasten off D. (8 ch-6 sps)

RND 9: With right side facing, join E with a sl st in any ch-6 sp, ch 3 (counts as dc), (dc, ch 1, 2 dc) in same sp, *ch 3, (3 dc, ch 3, 3 dc) in next sp (corner made), ch 3**, (2 dc, ch 1, 2 dc) in next sp, rep from * around, ending last rep at **, join with a sl st top of beg ch-3.

RND 10: Ch 1, sc in first st, sc in ch-1 sp, joining leaf, sc in each of next 2 sc, *2 sc in next ch-3 sp, sc in each of the next 3 dc, (2 sc, ch-2, 2 sc) next ch-3 sp (corner), sc in each of next 3 dc, 2 sc in next sp**, sc in each of the next 2 dc, joining leaf in last dc, sc in each of the next 2 dc, rep from * around, ending last rep at **, join with a sl st in first sc. Fasten off E. (4 of the 8 leaves joined at top)

RND 11: With right side facing, join B with a sl st in any corner ch-2 sp, ch 1, 2 sc in same corner sp, *sc in next 19 sc**, (2 sc, ch 2, 2 sc) in next corner ch-2 sp, rep from * around, ending last rep at **, 2 sc in same sp as beg corner, ch 2, join with a sl st in first sc to complete corner. Fasten off.

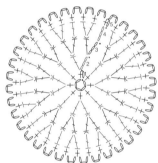

RNDS 1–5

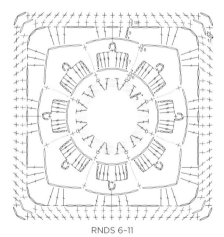

RNDS 6–11

SEPTEMBER MORNING GLORY

Morning glories symbolize love and affection.

SKILL LEVEL: Intermediate

Made with 5 colors: A, B, C, D, and E.

Picot: Ch 4, sc in 4th ch from hook.

Bpsc: Insert hook from back to front to back again around the post of next st, yo, draw through st, yo, draw through 2 loops on hook.

With A, ch 4, join with a sl st to form a ring.

RND 1: Ch 3 (counts as a dc here and throughout), dc in ring, [ch 1, 2 dc] 4 times in ring, ch 1, join with a sl st in top of beg ch-3. Fasten off A. (5 ch-1 sps 10 dc)

RND 2: With right side facing, join B in any ch-1 sp, ch 3 (dc, ch 2, 2 dc) in same sp, (2 dc, ch 2, 2 dc) in each ch-1 sp around, join with a sl st in top of beg ch-3. (5 shells)

RND 3: Sl st to first ch-2 sp, ch 3, 6 dc in same sp, 7 dc in each ch-2 sp around, join with a sl st top of beg ch-3. Fasten off B. (5 shells)

RND 4: With right side facing, join C in the first dc, ch 1, sc in first st, sc in next 6 dc, *working over sts in Rnd 3, dc in the sp between 2 shells in Rnd 2**, sc in each of next 7 dc, rep from * around, ending last rep at **, join with a sl st in the first sc. (35 sc, 5 dc)

RND 5: *Ch 5, skip next 7 sc, Bpsc around the post of the next dc, rep from * around, join with a sl st in first ch. Fasten off C. (5 ch-5 loops)

RND 6: With right side facing, join D with a sl st in any ch-5 sp, ch 1, [sc, hdc, dc, 3 tr, picot, 3 tr, dc, hdc, sc, ch 1] in each ch-5 loop around, join with a sl st in first sc. (5 petals)

RND 7: Working behind petals, *ch 7, sk next petal, sc in next ch-1 sp, rep from * around, join with a sl st in first ch. Fasten off D. (5 ch-7 loops)

RND 8: With right side facing, join E with a sl st in any ch-7 sp, ch 3, 7 dc in same sp, 8 dc in each ch-7 sp around, join with a sl st in top of beg ch-3. Fasten off E. (40 dc)

RND 9: With right side facing, join A with a sl st in any dc, ch 3, dc in each of the next 9 dc, ch 3 (corner), *dc in each of the next 10 dc, ch 3, rep from * around, join with a sl st in top of beg ch-3. Fasten off A. (10 dc on each side, 4 ch-3 corner sps)

RND 10: With right side facing, join B in any corner ch-3 sp, ch 1, *(2 sc, ch 2, 2 sc) in corner ch-3 sp, 1 sc in each of next 10 dc, rep from * around, join with a sl st in first sc. Fasten off B.

RND 11: With right side facing, join E in any corner ch-2 sp, ch 1, *(2 sc, ch 2, 2 sc) in corner ch-2 sp, sc in each of next 14 dc, rep from * around, join with a sl st in first sc. Fasten off.

OCTOBER MARIGOLD

Marigolds express joy and modesty.

SKILL LEVEL: Intermediate

Made with 5 colors: A, B, C, D, and E

Popcorn Stitch (PC): Work 5 dc in the same st, remove hook from last loop, insert hook into first of 5 dc, then back into working loop and draw loop through to form popcorn.

Picot: Ch 3, sl st in 3rd ch from hook.

With A, ch 4, join with a sl st to form a ring.

RND 1: Ch 1, 8 sc in ring, join with a sl st in first sc.

RND 2: Ch 1, 2 sc in each sc around (16 sc). Fasten off A.

Note: Petals are made alternating colors B and C, do not fasten off after each petal, carry yarn behind each petal to the next.

RND 3: With right side facing, join B with a sl st in any sc, *ch 6, sk 4 of the chs just made, work 5 dc in the 5th ch, sk next ch, sk next sc in Rnd 2, sl st in the next sc, drop B, pick up C in same st, ch 6, 5 dc in the 5th ch from hook, sk next ch, sk next sc in Rnd 2, sl st in next sc, drop C, alternating colors B and C, rep from * 3 times. Fasten off B. (8 petals)

RND 4: With C, working behind petals, ch 1, sc in first sl st, *ch 4, sk next petal, sc in sl st between petals, rep from * around, join with a sl st in first sc. Fasten off C. (8 ch-4 loops)

RND 5: With right side facing, join D with a sl st in any ch-4 loop, ch 1, (sc, hdc, dc, tr, picot, tr, dc, hdc, sc) in each ch-4 loop around, join with a sl st in first sc. (8 leaves)

RND 6: Working behind leaves, ch 1, sc in first sl st, *ch 4, sk next leaf**, sc between next 2 sc; rep from * around, ending last rep at **, join with a sl st in first sc. Fasten off D. (8 ch-4 loops)

RND 7: With right side facing, join E with a sl st in any ch-4 loop, ch 3 (counts as dc here and throughout), (2 dc, ch 3, 3 dc) in same loop (corner), *ch 2, 4 dc in next ch-4 loop, ch 2**, (3 dc, ch 3, 3 dc) in next ch-4 loop (corner), rep from * around, ending last rep at **, join with a sl st in top of beg ch-3. Fasten off E.

RND 8: With right side facing, join A, with a sl st in any corner ch-3 sp, ch 3, (2 dc, ch 3, 3 dc) in same ch-3 sp, *[ch 3, PC in next ch-2 sp] twice, ch 3**, (3 dc, ch 3, 3 dc) in next ch-3 corner sp, rep from * around, ending last rep at **, join with a sl st in top of beg ch-3. Fasten off A.

RND 9: With right side facing, join B with a sl st in any corner ch-3 sp, ch 1, *(2 sc, ch 2, 2 sc) in corner ch-3 sp, sc in each of the next 3 dc, [3 sc in next ch-3 sp, sc in next PC] twice, 3 sc in next ch-3 sp, sc in each of the next 3 dc, rep from * around, join with a sl st in first sc. Fasten off.

NOVEMBER CHRYSANTHEMUM

Chrysanthemum denotes cheerfulness, loveliness, and abundance.

SKILL LEVEL: Intermediate

Made with 5 colors: A, B, C, D, and E.

Picot: Ch 4, sl st in 4th ch from hook.

With A, ch 5, join with a sl st to form a ring.

RND 1: Ch 1, 12 sc in ring, join with a sl st in first sc.

RND 2: Working in front loops only, *ch 7, sc in 2nd ch from hook, sc in each ch across, sl st in next sc in Rnd 1, rep from * 11 times, join with a sl st to base of first petal. (12 petals)

RND 3: Working in the remaining back loops in Rnd 1, *ch 9, sc in 2nd ch from hook, sc in each ch across, sl st in next sc, rep from * 11 times, join with a sl st to base of first petal. Fasten off A. (12 petals)

RND 4: With right side facing, join B with a sl st in any sl st between petals, ch 1, sc in first st, *ch 3, sc in next sl st, rep from * around, join with a sl st in first sc. (12 ch-3 sps)

RND 5: *(Sc, 2 hdc, 2 dc, 2 tr, picot] in next ch-3 sp (2 trc, 2 dc, 2 hdc, sc) in next ch-3 sp, rep from * around, join with a sl st in first sc. (6 leaves)

RND 6: Working behind leaves, *ch 4, sc in sc at center of next leaf, ch 4, sc between next 2 leaves, rep from * around, join with a sl st in first sc. Fasten off B.

RND 7: With right side facing, join C in the sc between 2 leaves, ch 1, (2 sc, ch 2, 2 sc) in same st (corner), *[4 sc in next ch-4 sp, sc in next sc] twice, 4 sc in next ch-4 sp**, [2 sc, ch 2, 2 sc] next sc, rep from * around, ending last rep at **, join with a sl st in first sc.

RND 8: Sl st to next ch-2 sp, ch 3 (counts as dc), (dc, ch-2, 2 dc) in same sp (corner), *ch 1, sk next 2 sc, dc in each of the next 2 sc, [ch 2, sk 2 sc, dc in each of the next 2 sc] 3 times, ch 1, sk next 2 sc**, (2 dc, ch 2, 2 dc) in next ch-2 sp (corner), rep from * around, ending last rep at **, join with a sl st top of beg ch-3. Fasten off C.

RND 9: With right side facing, join D with a sl st in any corner ch-2 sp, ch 1, (2 sc, ch 2, 2 sc) in same sp, *[sc in each of next 2 dc, sc in next ch-sp] 5 times, sc in each of next 2 dc**, (2 sc, ch 2, 2 sc) in next corner ch-2 sp, rep from * around, ending last rep at **, join with a sl st in first sc. Fasten off D.

Center of Flower: With E, make a slip knot and place on hook, ch 1, work 10 sc into slip knot. Fasten off, leaving a sewing length. Tighten center ring. Sew in center of flower.

RNDS 1–3

RNDS 4–9

DECEMBER NARCISSUS

The Narcissus denotes respect, modesty, and faithfulness.

SKILL LEVEL: Experienced

Made with 4 colors: A, B, C, and D.

Joining leaf: To join leaf, place hook through point of leaf and through designated st or sp, pick up a loop, and complete a sc.

With A, make an adjustable ring.

RND 1: Ch 1, 10 sc in ring, join with a sl st in first sc, pull center loop tight.

RND 2: Working in front loops only, *ch 2, 3 hdc in next st, ch 2, sl st in next st, repeat from * around, join with a sl st. Fasten off A. (5 petals)

RND 3: Working in remaining back loops of sts in Rnd 1, with right side facing, join B with a sl st in any st in Rnd 1, ch 1, sc in same st, *ch 3, sc in next st, rep from *8 times, ch 3, sk next st, join with a sl st in first sc. (9 ch-3 sps)

RND 4: Ch 1 *(sc, dc, 3 tr, dc, sc) in each of next 2 loops, sc in next loop, rep from * twice, join with a sl st in first sc. (6 petals)

RND 5: Working behind petals, *ch 5, sc between the next 2 sc between petals, ch 5, sk next petal, sc in next sc between petals, rep from * around, join with a sl st in first ch of beg ch-5. Fasten off B. (6 ch-5 loops)

RND 6: With right side facing, join C with a sl st in any ch-5 loop, *(sc, hdc) in ch-5 loop, ch 8, sc in 2nd ch from hook, hdc in each of the next 6 ch, (hdc, sc) in same ch-5 loop of Rnd 5, rep from * around, join with a sl st in first sc. (6 leaves)

RND 7: Working behind leaves, *ch 3, sc in center of leaf in the ch-5 loop of Rnd 5, ch 3, sc between next 2 sc in Rnd 6, rep from * around, join with a sl st in first ch of first ch-3 sp. Fasten off C. (12 ch-3 sps)

(continued)

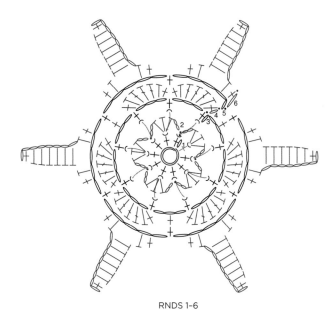

RNDS 1–6

RND 8: With right side facing, join D with a sl st in any ch-3 sp to the right of any leaf, ch 3, (2 dc, ch 3, 3 dc) in same sp (corner), *[ch 1, 3 dc in next ch-3 sp] twice, ch 1**, (3 dc, ch 3, 3 dc) in same sp (corner), rep from * around, ending last rep at **, join with a sl st in top of beg ch-3. Fasten off D.

RND 9: With right side facing, join A with a sl st in any corner ch-3 sp, ch 3, (dc, ch 2, 2 dc) in corner ch-3 sp, *[ch 2, 2 dc in next ch-1 sp] 3 times, ch 2**, (3 dc, ch 2, 3 dc) in next corner ch-3 sp, rep from * around, ending last rep at **, join with a sl st in top of beg ch-3.

RND 10: Sl st to next corner ch-2 sp, ch 1, *(2 sc, ch 2, 2 sc) in corner ch-3 sp, sc in each of next 2 dc, sc in next ch-2 sp, joining leaf, [sc in each of the next 2 dc, sc in next sp, sc in each of the next 2 dc, sc in next ch-2 sp] twice, sc in each of the next 2 dc, sc in next ch-2 sp, joining leaf, sc in each of next 2 dc, (2 sc, ch 2, 2 sc) in corner ch-3 sp, sc in each next 2 dc, sc in next ch-2 sp, sc in each of next 2 dc, sc in next ch-2 sp, joining leaf, [sc in each of the next 2 dc, sc in next ch-2 sp] twice, sc in each of next 2 dc, rep from * once, join with a sl st in first sc. Fasten off.

RNDS 7–10

BIRTHDAY FLOWER LAPGHAN

Every month has its own flower, and all twelve months are represented in this lapghan. You might prefer to make a gift for someone special using only their birthday month flower. Because some of the flower squares are very dimensional and colorful, and because I wanted them each to have their own space, I designed this small blanket with less showy April Daisies between them. You could also separate them with Classic Grannies (page 4).

Made with 14 colors

GRANNY SQUARES

Make one each of the Flowers of the Month.

JANUARY CARNATION: Pink (A), Kelly Green (B), Dusty Green (C)

FEBRUARY VIOLET: Colonial Blue (A), Kelly Green (B), Fern (C), Dusty Purple (D)

MARCH DAFFODIL: Radiant Yellow (A), Kelly Green (B), Fern (C)

APRIL DAISY: Radiant Yellow (A), White (B), Kelly Green (C), Fern (D)

MAY LILY OF THE VALLEY: (Use G hook for this square) Kelly Green (A), Dusty Green (B), Espresso (C), White (D)

JUNE ROSE: Scarlet (A), Kelly Green (B), Dusty Green (C)

JULY WATER LILY: Radiant Yellow (A), White (B), Kelly Green (C), Dusty Purple (D)

AUGUST POPPY: Radiant Orange (A), Espresso (B), Scarlet (C), Dusty Green (D), Toffee (E)

SEPTEMBER MORNING GLORY: White (A), Purple (B), Colonial Blue (C), Dusty Green (D), Kelly Green (E)

YARN Worsted weight #4

Shown: Lion Brand Vanna's Choice, 100% acrylic , 170 yd (56 m), 3.5 oz (100 g), 1 skein each of White 100, Pink 101, Colonial Blue 109, Scarlet 113, Toffee 124, Espresso 127, Radiant Orange 132, Brick 133, Dusty Purple 146, Radiant Yellow 157, Mustard 158, 2 skeins each of Fern 171, Dusty Green 173, Kelly Green 172

HOOK Size H/8 (5 mm) and G/6 (4 mm) (used only for May Square)

GAUGE Each square = 6" (15 cm); 6 mesh sts (1 dc, ch-1 between) = 4" (10 cm)

NOTIONS Yarn needle

SIZE 38" x 38" (96.5 x 96.5 cm)

SKILL LEVEL Intermediate

OCTOBER MARIGOLD: Mustard (A), Brick (B), Pink (C), Kelly Green (D), Fern (E)

NOVEMBER CHRYSANTHEMUM: Radiant Yellow (A), Kelly Green (B), Fern (C), Espresso (D), Toffee (E)

DECEMBER NARCISSUS: Radiant Yellow (A), White (B), Kelly Green (C), Dusty Green (D)

Make 13 April Daisy Squares with Dusty Green (A) and (B), Kelly Green (C), Fern (D).

When all squares are made, sew them together from the wrong side, using back loops only, following Assembly Diagram on page 30 for flower placement.

BORDER

RND 1: With Fern, Join with a sl st in any corner sp, 2 sc in same sp (half corner made) * Work 120 sc along one side of blanket, having 20 sc in each square ** (2 sc, ch 2, 2 sc) in corner sp, rep from * twice, rep from * to ** once, 2 sc, ch 2, in same corner as joining, join with a sl st to beg sc.

RND 2: Fern, ch 3 (cts as dc) 1 dc slightly back in the corner sp (half corner made) *[Ch 2, sk 2 sc, 1 dc in next sc] 41 times, ch 2, sk 1 sc ** (2 dc, ch 3, 2 dc) in next corner ch-2 space (42 ch-2 spaces) rep from * twice, rep from * to ** once, 2 dc, ch 3 in same corner as beg, join to 3rd ch of beg ch-3.

RND 3: Fern, ch 3, 2 dc in same corner (half corner made) * ch 2, sk 1 dc, 1 dc in next dc [ch 2, 1 dc in next dc] 42 times, ch 2, sk 1 dc** (3 dc, ch 3, 3 dc) in next corner ch-3 sp (44 ch 2 sp) rep from * twice, rep from * to ** once, 3 dc, ch 3 in the same corner sp as beg, join to the 3rd ch of beg ch-3 to complete corner.

RND 4: Fern, ch 3, 2 dc in same corner sp (half corner made) *ch-2, sk 2 dc, 1 dc in next dc [ch 2, 1 dc in next dc] 44 times, ch 2, sk 2 dc **(3 dc, ch 3, 3 dc) in corner ch-3 space (46 ch-2 spaces), rep from * twice, rep from * to ** once, 3 dc, ch 3 in same corner sp as beg, join with a sl st to 3rd ch of beg ch-3.

RND 5: Fern, ch 3, 2 dc in same corner sp (half corner made) *ch-2, sk 2 dc, 1 dc in next dc [ch 2, 1 dc in next dc] 46 times, ch 2, sk 2 dc **(3 dc, ch 3, 3 dc) in corner ch-3 space (48 ch-2 spaces), rep from * twice, rep from * to ** once, 3 dc, ch 3 in same corner sp as beg, join with a sl st to 3rd ch of beg ch-3, fasten off Fern.

RND 6: Join Dusy Purple with a sl st in any corner sp, * ch 5, sk 2 dc, 1 sc in next dc [ch 5, sk next dc, 1 sc in next dc] 24 times, ch 5, 1 sc in corner sp (26 ch-5 spaces), rep from * 3 times more, end last rep sl st in the beg sl st.

RND 7: Dusty Purple, work 7 sc in each ch-5 sp around, end with a sl st to the first sc, fasten off Dusty Purple.

RND 8: Join Kelly Green with a sl st in any corner, working from the back loop, sk 1 sc *1 sc in each of next 3 sc, ch 3, 1 sc in same sc as ch-3 (picot made), 1 sc in each of the next 2 sc, sk 2 sc, rep from * all around, join with a sl st to beg sl st, fasten off.

FINISHING

If desired, using same color yarn, working from the wrong side, tack down some of the larger petals/leaves.

BLOCKING

Place on a padded surface, pin into shape, spray with water and pat gently into shape. Do not iron.

ASSEMBLY DIAGRAM

A	JAN	A	MAY	A
DEC	A	JUN	A	FEB
A	APR	A	JUL	A
AUG	A	SEP	A	OCT
A	NOV	A	MAR	A

ABBREVIATIONS

Here is the list of standard abbreviations used for crochet.

approx	approximately	**FPdc**	front post double crochet	**Sl st**	slip stitch
beg	begin/beginning	**FPsc**	front post single crochet	**sp(s)**	space(s)
bet	between	**g**	gram(s)	**st(s)**	stitch(es)
BL	back loop(s)	**hdc**	half double crochet	**tbl**	through back loop(s)
bo	bobble	**inc**	increase/increases/increasing	**tch**	turning chain
BP	back post	**lp(s)**	loop(s)	**tfl**	through front loop(s)
BPdc	back post double crochet	**Lsc**	long single crochet	**tog**	together
BPsc	back post single crochet	**m**	meter(s)	**tr**	triple crochet
CC	contrasting color	**MC**	main color	**trtr**	triple treble crochet
ch	chain	**mm**	millimeter(s)	**tr2tog**	triple crochet 2 stitches together
ch-	refers to chain or space previously made, e.g., ch-1 space	**oz**	ounce(s)	**WS**	wrong side(s)
ch lp	chain loop	**p**	picot	**yd**	yard(s)
ch-sp	chain space	**patt**	pattern	**yo**	yarn over
CL	cluster(s)	**pc**	popcorn	**[ ]**	Work instructions within brackets as many times as directed
cm	centimeter(s)	**pm**	place marker		
cont	continue	**prev**	previous	**( )**	Work instructions within prentheses as many times as directed
dc	double crochet	**rem**	remain/remaining		
dc2tog	double crochet 2 stitches together	**rep**	repeat(s)	*****	Repeat instructions following the single asterisk as directed
dec	decrease/decreases/decreasing	**rev sc**	reverse single crochet		
dtr	double triple	**rnd(s)**	round(s)	*** ***	Repeat instructions between asterisks as many times as directed or repeat from a given set of instructions
FL	front loop(s)	**RS**	right side(s)		
foll	follow/follows/following	**sc**	single crochet		
FP	front post	**sc2tog**	single crochet 2 stitches together		
		sk	skip		

SYMBOLS
STITCH KEY

⌒ = chain (ch)
• = slip stitch (Sl st)
✝ = single crochet (sc)
T = half double crochet (hdc)
T = double crochet (dc)
T = treble crochet (tr)
T = double treble crochet (dtr)
✝ = long sc (LSC)
✝ = long dc (LDC)
L = long treble crochet (LTR)
T = front post treble crochet (FPtr)

V or V = V-st
X = crossed dc
= Berry Stitch (BS)
= petal st
= sc2tog
= dc5tog
= tr2tog
or = puff st
= cluster (3 dc)
= beg cluster (3 dc)

= 2-tr cluster, tr2tog
= 3-tr cluster, tr3tog
= beginning popcorn (beg PC)
= 5-dc popcorn st (PC)
= mock popcorn st (MPC)
= bubble st (BS)
= various picots
= worked in back loop only
= worked in front loop only
= make join
= adjustable ring